For Mac, Always

ALPENGLOW

ALPENGLOW

CREATIVE CELEBRATIONS FOR EVERY SEASON

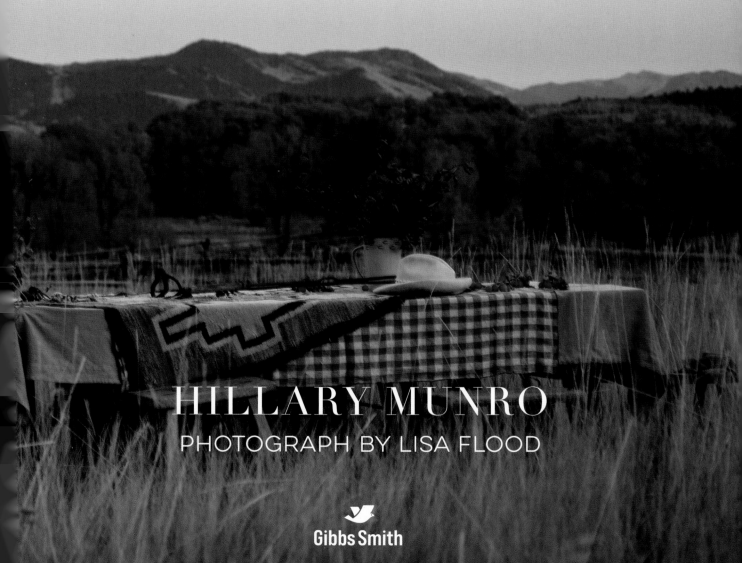

HILLARY MUNRO

PHOTOGRAPH BY LISA FLOOD

Gibbs Smith

Introduction

al·pen·glow /ˈalpənˌglō/ the rosy light of the setting or rising sun seen on high mountains

Alpenglow is the magic hour when the sky turns shades of pink and orange not found on a color wheel, an experience that happens often in the mountains, regardless of the season, that fills your soul with a moment of joy.

After being uprooted from an easy suburban life as a young, enthusiastic, and brave teenager, I landed in a tiny cowboy ski town in the American West, where my new home was surrounded by the natural world. I wasn't comfortable in this land where winter can last half the year. But when I observed the locals dressed in layers of synchilla and ranch gear, giant waterproof boots, and with paisley-print silk scarfs wrapped around their necks, they made this way of life look effortless, even romantic.

I soon fell in love with mountain living, embracing the seasons, nature, and a simpler way of living. We feel seasonality deeply in mountains, which keeps me grounded and rooted to the earth. The season dictates what I serve for meals, how I set my table, which flowers I use, and what rituals I follow year after year.

Winter is filled with the smell of wood smoke, wool blankets, and hearty stews. Spring restores possibilities, when the snow melts and garden beds are prepped, lighter colors add cheer to our plates, and the horses come home from winter pasture. Summer breathes freedom with a loose schedule and endless hours outside by rivers, with casual picnics and lemonade. Fall is a reflective time, when things slow down, we enjoy garden abundance, chop firewood, play backgammon, and fill the pantry with jars for the winter.

Without question, food brings people together. Dragging a table to an unexpected location, such as a field or by a river, creates an atmosphere that guests will remember long after the meal is finished. I look to nature for inspiration when planning any celebration, whether for a crowd or my family. Foraging on a hike or in the backyard is an easy and inexpensive way to incorporate the natural world at the table.

One afternoon in late fall, I set a table in front of a fire in my backyard. On a hike earlier in the day, I had stumbled upon some beautiful sagebrush that I wanted to incorporate into our party. From the time I was a little girl, my grandmother and mother taught me to make things by hand, so I decided to combine the sagebrush and other foraged items into little bundles. I gathered some dishes my grandmother had given me and set a casual table. I placed a handmade smudge bundle with an intention card on each plate. When the evening was coming to an end, we burned our intentions in the fire as the sky turned pink.

In *Alpenglow*, I invite you into my world of creatively celebrating the four seasons. I share authentic ways for setting an outdoor table in unexpected places, making things with your hands, and living an inspired life through stories, newfound traditions, family, and a little magic.

Winter Season of Quiet

Wintering is quiet and long in this season of unapologetic rigor. Being in the wildness of Mother Nature is what makes this white season particularly magical. The intense storms swirl and bluster, balanced by days of soft and peaceful calm. A crackling fire is a daily ritual for warmth and ambience. Candlelight suppers make the mundane weeknights feel like celebrations. This is the season of social darkness, when a get-together with friends feels rich and meaningful, with fragrant pots of food slowly simmering on the range all day. This time of quiet making—working with my hands, experimenting with preserves, dipping and pouring candles, planting paperwhites, and sewing—fills my soul. Urgency is less relevant now than in other seasons, so there are private moments for daydreaming. Winter generates a rhythm of restoration, silent purpose, and quiet reflection.

Winter Rituals

Bundle up and go outside

Forage winter greens and mossy branches

Slow dance in the kitchen

Drink hot cocoa

Go sledding

Read an old book out loud to the family

Take long baths

Smile at a stranger

Write a love note and mail it

Play cards

Build puzzles in front of the fire

Cut down a Christmas tree

Make a gingerbread house

Visit the library

Have a bonfire in the snow

Make a snow angel

Ice skate on a frozen lake

Do the Polar Plunge

Listen to the snow fall

Create things with your hands

Set intentions for the new year

Shovel snow

Foraging

Winter foraging, while quite monochromatic with greens being the primary color palette, challenges me. I love the hunt and adventure as well as the peace and the quiet the woods provide. I am inspired by the natural shapes that spark my creativity. Unusual colors of various shades are an inspiration for me.

I am always on the hunt for junipers with plump lavender berries and messy mossy branches. I carry an oversized basket and head up the ski-packed Forest Service trail with my sharpest pruners in hand. I am inspired by the quiet, and roam around the forest until something piques my interest. Pine cones, dried hawthorn berries, and other interesting pods that haven't been buried by the snow are always collected. In pursuit of the perfect branch, I often lose myself, ending up waist deep in snow, or other times reaching for a pine cone–studded branch on a fir tree and being enchanted by a bird singing a song. Sometimes I get lucky and find a feather, antler, or bone. When my basket is full and I am confident that I have collected enough material to decorate for tonight's gathering, I head down the snow-covered road towards home.

Assembling foraged materials can take the form of an abstract arrangement in a vessel. First, find an oversized container. You can stabilize the greens by using chicken wire or floral foam. Begin by placing the most robust greens in and then build upon it by adding mossy branches in various directions. Place the delicate berries last.

Winter Gatherings

Using décor elements that play on the season of hibernation will set the tone for your winter gatherings. I embrace the moody, dark evenings by using richer colors, Pendleton blankets, hides, dark-colored candles, and mismatched vintage candleholders. I stuff foraged greens into large planters and use them throughout my home during the winter months. They look chic, are inexpensive, and are an easy way to bring nature inside. You can create a beautiful centerpiece by laying the foraged greens down the center of the table as a base, creating a deconstructed garland. Build on the garland by nestling in things like pots or vases of forced winter bulbs, seasonal fruits, or unique winter flowers from the market. One of my favorite things to do is drape my chandeliers with vines of dried hops. They are easy to work with, have beautiful flowers, and keep their sturdy shape when dried.

Wreath Making in the Cabin

A few years ago, I began hosting wreath-making workshops in our little cabin that lives in the backyard. The event has become a wonderful tradition for gathering friends, old and new. I keep wreaths hanging in our home year-round, but the holidays are a particularly fun time to build something you can enjoy all winter. There is no right way to make a wreath, but here are some tips that will ensure satisfaction.

Supplies

Wreath frame

Various greens, including spruce, fir, juniper, cedar, boxwood

Green paddle wire

Clippers

Hot glue gun

Ribbon

Other options: eucalyptus, snowberries, dried flowers, sage, ilex berries, lotus pods, pine cones, dried oranges, thistle, feather, an antler

First, you need a base (I prefer a wire frame or a grapevine wreath). Next, gather your materials and decide on the color palette for your project. Start by wiring your robust greens to the frame and, working in a circle, continue attaching the greens to form your base. Tuck, wire, or glue your decorations in place. If possible, hang the wreath on a wall to see if there are any holes or if you need to add any accents. Add the ribbon as the finishing touch.

Classic Swiss Fondue

Serves 4

1 garlic clove, halved

1 cup dry white wine

1 pound Gruyère cheese, grated

1/2 pound Emmentaler cheese, grated

1 tablespoon plus 1 teaspoon cornstarch

1 teaspoon fresh lemon juice

Freshly grated nutmeg

Rub the inside of a fondue pot or cast-iron skillet with the garlic clove. Warm the wine in the pot. Add the cheeses, cornstarch, and lemon juice. Cook over medium heat, stirring occasionally, until the cheeses begin to melt, about 5 minutes. Reduce heat to low. Add nutmeg and cook, stirring gently, for another 3 minutes. Serve with bread, salami, pears, and apples.

Christmas Tree Hunt

The hunt to find our Christmas tree is one of my favorite days of the year. It marks the beginning of the holiday season and a focus on making and giving. I like to put our tree up the day after Thanksgiving and keep it up well past New Year's. This year we decide to head south to the Hoback Canyon. I dust off the wooden handle of our Dandy saw, grab two faded blue Cam straps, and pack up a warm picnic to satisfy hunger and thirst for the day of tromping through the woods.

When we arrive, Mac heads west up the hillside through punchy powder; the kids and I follow up the boot pack he has stomped down in the snow. The common alpine trees here are prickly blue spruces, commanding lodgepole pines, and friendly firs. In nature, trees grow clustered together, resulting in one pretty side and one barren side. This adds to the difficulty of finding the perfect tree. But we decide on a beautiful lodgepole and haul it down the mountain.

After heaving the tree into the back of the truck and strapping down the branches, it's time to enjoy our energy-boosting picnic of chestnut soup, beet-dyed deviled eggs, and hot chocolate. This is a great way to celebrate the start of the magical season.

Chestnut Soup

Serves 4–6

4 tablespoons unsalted butter

1/2 medium onion , finely chopped

1 medium carrot, finely chopped

1 celery rib, finely chopped

2 cups cooked chestnuts from 1 (14.8)-ounce vacuum-packed jar

1 cup port wine

3 cups chicken stock

2 sprigs fresh thyme

1/2 cup heavy cream

Salt and freshly ground pepper, to taste

Melt the butter in a medium skillet. Add the onion, carrot, and celery and cook over medium-low heat, stirring until softened, about 10 minutes. Add the chestnuts and cook for another 5 minutes. Add the port and cook over medium-high heat until the port is reduced by half, about 5 minutes. Add the stock and thyme sprigs; bring to a boil. Cover partially and simmer over low heat for 30 minutes. Discard the thyme and add the cream. Working in batches, purée the soup in a blender. Return soup to the saucepan and bring to a simmer. Season with salt and pepper and serve.

Beet-Dyed Deviled Eggs

Makes 24 halves

1 large beet

2 cups water

1 cup white vinegar

12 hard-cooked eggs, peeled

1/4 cup mayonnaise

2 tablespoons sweet pickle relish

1 tablespoon whole grain mustard

Coarse salt and ground pepper

Wash, peel, and cube the beet. Place in a medium saucepan with water and vinegar; bring to boiling. Reduce heat and simmer, covered, for 15 minutes. Remove from heat; set aside to cool completely, but do not drain.

Place the eggs in the saucepan with the beet and liquid. Let stand for 10 to 15 minutes. Remove from liquid and slice the eggs in half; discard the beet and liquid. Remove the yolk and set the whites aside. Combine the yolks with mayonnaise, relish, mustard, and a pinch of salt. Scoop filling back into egg white halves. Sprinkle with salt and pepper.

Hot Chocolate To Go A Gift

Makes 4 (8-ounce) jars

Hot Chocolate To Go is an easily assembled gift for any occasion: a simple hostess gift, a sweet treat for a teacher, or for guests. Layer the ingredients in a glass jar to make them shine. Begin with the hot chocolate mix then add a layer of marshmallows; add the shaved chocolate bar, and top with crushed candy cane. Tie the gift with a piece of holiday fabric or festive ribbon.

Supplies

Glass jars with fitted lids

2 cups hot chocolate mix

2 cups small marshmallows

2 milk chocolate bars, shaved

4 large candy canes, crushed

Holiday ribbon or fabric

Ice Fishing Expedition

On a chilly January morning, we gather friends and pack the back of the truck with a heavy grill grate, firewood, warm jackets, and a cooler of food to spend the day on a frozen lake at the base of the Gros Ventre Range to do some ice fishing with friends. The sun is forecast to shine today, but that has yet to happen.

After driving miles down a snowy, pot-hole-ridden road, we veer towards Slide Lake, a lake created by a landslide in 1929, which formed a dam that eventually broke and flooded the tiny cowboy-hippie town of Kelly below. During the summer months, the lake swells with paddle boarders, fishermen, and campers. In the winter, the lake freezes and is used by ice skaters, ice fisherman, and snowmobilers, who have access to miles of terrain just behind the gate where the road is not maintained in the winter. We had little expectation of catching any lake trout, but the fish were surprisingly abundant, making our picnic a crowd favorite.

Fire-Grilled Oysters

Nothing is more unconventional and unexpected for a gathering of friends than a fire on a frozen lake with fresh grilled oysters.

Serves 8 to 10

2 dozen fresh oysters

2 lemons

Tarragon Butter (see recipe below)

Sliced French baguette, grilled

Build a fire outdoors in a safe spot, with a heavy metal grate for roasting. Maintain the heat and fire until the coals are red hot.

Place the fresh oysters on the grill (I wear leather gloves) cup side down so the flat part of the shell is facing up, to preserve the oyster liquid. After each oyster shell begins to open, pry the top shell off using an oyster knife and discard, leaving oysters with their liquid in the shell. Add a small slice of tarragon butter and let it melt in the oyster shell. When cool, they are ready to slurp. *Be careful, though: the shells get incredibly hot.* Butter a slice of baguette and top with grilled oysters for a heartier bite.

Tarragon Butter

Yields 1 butter loaf

1 bunch fresh tarragon, chopped

2 sticks unsalted butter, room temperature

2 garlic cloves, minced

Zest of 2 lemons

Salt and pepper

Place the butter, tarragon, garlic, lemon zest, and salt and pepper in a bowl. Combine the ingredients together using a fork.

Place the butter compound in the center of a piece of unbleached parchment paper. Fold the paper to cover the butter. Roll the butter into a tight cylinder. Twist the ends to encase the butter and secure with string or a rubber band.

Butter will keep in the fridge for a week or in the freezer for up to 6 months.

Herby Fire Trout

This is a favorite appetizer served on butter crackers, or over pasta as a main course.

Makes 4 small portions

1 whole trout

2 tablespoons minced fresh parsley, rosemary, and dill

2 cloves garlic, minced

4 tablespoons olive oil or butter, divided

2 lemons, sliced in circles

Pepper and Maldon sea salt, to taste

Parsley, minced, for finishing

Fresh lemon juice

In a small bowl mix together the parsley, rosemary, dill, and garlic with 2 tablespoons of olive oil or butter. Spread evenly inside the cavity of the cleaned trout. Add a thick layer of lemon slices over the herb mixture, then sprinkle with salt and pepper. Wrap the fish in foil and cool for up to two hours. You can keep it cold on the ice or in the refrigerator.

Heat your grate or barbecue grill to high heat; then reduce to medium. Place the fish packet over medium heat and cook for 5 to 7 minutes per side. If it is a large fish, increase the cooking time. Remove the fish carefully from the heat and open the foil. Sprinkle the cavity with fresh parsley, remaining oil or butter, and fresh lemon juice. Use a fork to scrape the meat and herbs off the bones.

Winter Sleigh Feed

In 1905 the Linn family, driving a team of horses from North Dakota, stopped in Jackson Hole, Wyoming, because their wagon wheel broke on Teton Pass. While waiting for repairs, they found one of the last pieces of land to homestead in Wilson, Wyoming, and never left. I met the Linns—Gene, Ellen, Peter, and Laura—when I moved to Jackson Hole in 1992. They are fourth-generation outfitters and ranchers, a family who knows every mountain and valley on either side of the Tetons.

When the opportunity arose to feed the Linns' horses and cows from the back of a horse-drawn sleigh, I jumped at the chance to introduce my kids to this western tradition. In deep snow, the Linns feed hay from a sleigh once a day.

On a chilly afternoon, we followed Laura's husband, Dwayne, to the hitching rail, where we met Norman and Handy, the Linns' twenty-three-year-old draft horses. Dwayne and his father-in-law, Gene, proceeded to tack up the team with black-and-silver harnesses from a shed crowded with old mounts, a bucket of moose feed, and wooden panniers. When the horses had been hooked to the sleigh, Laura took the reins and the rest of us piled in the back. As the team and sleigh lurched forward and the harnesses jangled, we grabbed onto the orange twine securing the hay bales and set off down a snowy lane.

From the moving sleigh, we distributed hay in piles to the horses. We didn't need to be precise when we fed the cows, so we tossed the hay quickly, creating a tornado of loose greens. We passed by the Tetons and along a semi-frozen pond where swans fed. The kids helped with the gates and took turns steering. Upon returning to the barnyard, everyone helped untack Norman and Handy and turn them back into their corral. As the sun was setting, we enjoyed a picnic of ranch beans and cider while a crew of ranch pups gathered around our ankles.

Ranch Beans

An aromatic pot of beans simmering on the stove is one of winter's best meals. When I was growing up, my mom simmered beans on the stove during the winter months, which inspired me to make this hearty dish. You can scoop them over rice or cornbread or simply serve them on their own.

Serves 8–10

1 cup dry kidney beans

1/4 teaspoon baking soda

3 garlic gloves, minced

1 small white onion, diced

1 tablespoon tomato paste

3 cups boiling water, divided

1/2 teaspoon ground cumin

1/2 teaspoon Italian seasoning

1/2 teaspoon dried mint

1/2 teaspoon salt, plus more to taste

1/4 teaspoon freshly ground black pepper

Pick over the beans and remove any pebbles or other debris. Soak them in a pot with water to cover for at least 8 hours or overnight. Add the baking soda to the soaking beans to help make them easier to digest.

Drain and rinse the beans. In a large pot, sauté the garlic with onions until translucent. Add the tomato paste and stir together. Add 1 cup of boiling water. Stir in the prepared beans, all seasonings, and remaining water. Simmer uncovered for 45 minutes.

Baking Powder Biscuits

A family favorite made from my grandmother Jackie's recipe inspired by one in the Doubleday cookbook from the 1920s.

Makes 12 biscuits

3 cups all-purpose flour

1 teaspoon salt

1 tablespoon baking powder

1 tablespoon sugar

6 tablespoons butter, room temperature

1 to 1 1/8 cups cold milk or buttermilk

Preheat oven to 425 degrees and move a rack to the upper third of the oven. Line a baking sheet with parchment paper. Mix together the flour, salt, baking powder, and sugar.

Work the butter into the flour mixture using a stand mixer (or your hands); your goal is an evenly crumbled mixture.

Drizzle a small amount of milk evenly over the flour mixture. Mix quickly and gently for about 15 seconds, until you have a cohesive dough. If the mixture seems dry and won't come together, add more milk incrementally.

Place the dough on a lightly floured work surface. Shape it into a rough rectangle about 3/4 inch thick. Fold it into thirds like a letter and roll gently with a floured rolling pin until the dough is 3/4 inch thick again. Cut the dough into 2-inch squares with a sharp knife. Place the biscuits bottom side up on your prepared baking sheet. Brush the biscuits with milk to enhance browning.

Bake the biscuits for 15 to 20 minutes, until lightly browned. Remove them from the oven and serve warm.

Galloping Goodies Horse Treats

My mom developed this recipe as a way to reuse the spent grain from the brewpub my family founded. She sold the horse cookies at our local farmers market.

Makes 30 (2-inch) treats

1/2 cup grated carrots

2 cups cooked barley

1 cup cracked corn

2 cups rolled oats

2 cups oat bran

1 cup whole-wheat flour

1 1/4 cups apple juice

1/2 cup molasses, more as needed

1 1/3 cups all-purpose flour

Preheat oven to 350 degrees. Have 2 cookie sheets ready. In a large bowl, combine all ingredients, adding more molasses if needed for the mixture to stick together. Form 2-inch discs. Place on cookie sheets one inch apart. Bake treats for 20 minutes; then rotate and cook another 20 minutes. Let dry overnight before packaging.

Spring Season of Reawakening

Spring is a dynamic time where daily changes are noticeable. I wait for the snow to melt each year, desperate for color to enter the realm after a blanket of white has graced the valley floor for months. Shed hunting is a spring ritual where locals scurry to the hills on horseback or on ATVs in search of antler treasures dropped by moose, elk, and deer as soon as winter closures put in place to protect animals from human-caused exertion have lifted. I incorporate antlers into my tablescapes, floral arrangements, and as an organic element in my home.

Finally, we can put away the skis, pack boots, and down and replace them with muddy muck boots, rain jackets, and worn-in wool flannels.

Reflections of the snowcapped mountains in puddles are magic. The trees begin to bud and sprout green, the birds quietly migrate back, and animals emerge after the hibernation season. Because of our altitude, spring doesn't seem to come until May, which is when we see bulbs breaking through the ground and rhubarb sprouting in the garden soil.

Spring cleaning is daunting. I look outside to find broken chairs that didn't survive the weight of the winter. The grass is matted with lost socks, garden tools, and dog toys.

The neighborhood ice rink turns into a rodeo arena, and straw hats replace our beanies. Everyone is eager to get the seeds started and plant their gardens, but to be safe, locals wait until June 1 to set out plants, as there is much less likely to be a hard freeze after this date. We have a very short growing season, with only 90 frost-free days, so time is of the essence.

Spring Rituals

Hold a baby chicken

Hunt for a shed treasure

Old West Days Parade

Watch the strutting grouse

See the first robin

Stop and look at the baby cows

Find an abandoned bird's nest and use it as décor

Plant vegetable seeds

Prepare the garden

Notice bulbs sprouting

Read poems aloud after dinner

Put winter away

Clean out a closet

Dye eggs

Clean up tack and bring the horses home

Find fresh tulips at a local farm

Cook the last of winter preserves

Rake the yard

Look for rhubarb

Open all the windows in the house

Eat outside regardless of the weather

Keeping a Few Chickens

We have had chickens for a few years. Most mornings, the kids grab the enamelware bucket with food scraps and, regardless of the season, walk out to the coop to give the girls their morning snack. The kids collect the beautiful blue, green, olive, and brown eggs and put them in a basket on the kitchen counter.

Many communities allow chickens now, and having acreage is not necessarily important. Backyard coops are popping up everywhere, including cities and schoolyards. Carla, Grassy, and Scrappy were our first Buff Orpington hens. They are easy keepers in our harsh climate, and they entertain us with their unique personalities. They eat much of our household food and garden waste; managing them teaches my children responsibility for taking care of animals. We love to use our fresh eggs for making pies and include them in daily cooking as well. There are often enough to share with treasured friends and neighbors; we get creative with branding the cartons, giving these deliveries a special touch.

Spring Gatherings

Spring calls for lightening things up, and I strive to incorporate this way of thinking in the foods I prepare and how I set the table. Foraging for budding lilac branches on a neighborhood tree and cutting a few peony stems brings color to the table and contributes a wonderful fragrance.

I decided to set this over-the-top spring table at our nursery as inspiration for our customers. Our shop is especially stimulating in the spring because people are starved for color and enjoy being surrounded by things that are growing. I found a dusty stack of floral dishes at a vintage shop nearby, and they added a granny chic element. These types of dishes are readily found at antique or junk malls and can be mix and matched, adding an inexpensive touch of whimsy to your outdoor celebration.

Hot Springs Excursion

We met in the morning before work for our annual spring soak, breaking up the mundane work week. Tromping down the trail to these riverside pools is a ritual that marks the end of winter. Before the banks of the river rise with winter runoff and the frozen water has thawed, a natural hot spring is revealed. The air temperature on this day was in the single digits, making a quick plunge in the icy cold river seem unthinkable, but the reward was the tingle of the 105 plus–degree water on our skin. After our soak, we enjoyed a cup of cowboy coffee that I had brewed ahead and gobbled up classic scones while warming in wool Pendleton blankets. We parted for work invigorated by hot water, friendship, and conversation.

If you don't have a hot spring nearby, you can easily re-create this ritual by meeting a friend outdoors for a nature walk, a cup of coffee on a park bench, or a quick dip in some cold water.

Cowboy Coffee

Cowboy coffee was so named because it had to be simple and made in large batches for a crew of cowboys on the trail. This classic western way of making coffee is similar to making French press coffee. I always make mine in an old enamelware pot. These are easily found at antique stores; just make sure to check for holes in the pot before purchasing.

Makes 1 pot

1/4 cup ground coffee (any brand will do)

1 quart warm water

Fill the pot with warm water, add the coffee grounds, and bring to a rolling boil. Boil for about 4 minutes. Hint: the longer it boils the stronger the coffee will be.

Remove the pot from the heat and let it sit for two minutes. Add a dash of cold water or egg shells to help settle the grounds. Gently pour into cups and enjoy.

Classic Scones with Huckleberry Jam

These hearty scones are perfect topped with jam and butter or cream. You can wrap them in foil to keep them warm if venturing out on a cold morning.

Makes 8–10

2 cups cake flour

1/2 teaspoon kosher salt

2 teaspoons baking powder

3 tablespoons sugar, divided

5 tablespoons unsalted butter, cut into pieces

1 egg

1/2 cup heavy cream, divided

Crème fraîche (optional)

Huckleberry jam (optional)

Preheat oven to 450 degrees F.

Place the flour, salt, baking powder, and 2 tablespoons of the sugar in a food processor fit with a paddle attachment; pulse until combined. Add the butter and pulse until the mixture resembles cornmeal. Add the egg and just enough cream to form a slightly sticky dough. If it's too sticky, add a touch of flour—it should still stick to your hands.

Place the dough on a lightly floured surface and knead once or twice. Press the dough into a 3/4-inch-thick circle and cut into 2-inch rounds with a biscuit cutter or water glass. Put the rounds an inch apart on an ungreased baking sheet. Gently reshape the leftover dough and cut again. Brush the top of each scone with a bit of cream and sprinkle with a little of the remaining sugar. Bake for 9 to 11 minutes, or until the scones are beautifully golden brown. Serve immediately with your choice of toppings.

Fishing Picnic

Few things are more romantic than a picnic on the banks of a creek. Add fly-fishing and delicious food with friends and it turns into an afternoon of memories. You can easily pack a small picnic and make it special by elevating the experience. For example, bring something nice to sit on—a stool, blanket, or chair. Using environmentally friendly and reusable vessels and wrapping sandwiches in paper is a modern take on basic plasticware. For a rewarding repast, I pack something unexpected that is easily transported in a basket. A favorite beverage is a sloshy, which is basically an adult slushy; delis and gas stations all over town sell them, but some are better than others. I make mine with healthier fresh ingredients and a liquor that pairs well. For this afternoon picnic. I paired my homemade raspberry grapefruit sloshy with gourmet sandwiches of tomato jam, salty prosciutto, and thick slices of fresh mozzarella. I also packed an orzo pasta salad, chips, and snap peas to round out the meal. As a favor, I brought some hand-tied flies made by a friend and local fishing guide.

Tomato Jam

This tomato jam is sweet and tart and pairs beautifully with thick slices of mozzarella cheese and cured meats. The clove and cinnamon add a holiday element that is unexpected out of the season.

Makes 2 cups

1 pound Roma tomatoes, cored and chopped

1 cup sugar

2 tablespoon fresh lime juice

1 tablespoon grated ginger

1 teaspoon ground cumin

1/4 teaspoon cinnamon

1/8 teaspoon cloves

Pinch of salt

1 jalapeño, seeded and minced

Combine all the ingredients in a heavy saucepan and bring to a boil over medium heat, stirring often. Reduce the heat to a low simmer and stir occasionally until the consistency is thick like jam. This usually takes about an hour. Taste and adjust seasonings then cool and refrigerate. Jam will last for up to a week.

Raspberry Grapefruit Sloshy

The go-to summer beverage in Jackson is this sweet and slightly sour frosty drink. It's refreshing after a hike, on the river, or at a picnic. Transport the drink in any thermos and serve it in enamelware cups. The drink can alternatively be made without alcohol for a fresh, cold mocktail.

Makes 4 drinks

2 cups frozen raspberries

2 cups fresh-squeezed grapefruit juice

1 cup ice cubes

1/3 cup sugar

1 cup Tito's vodka, optional

Combine all the ingredients in a blender or food processor then divide among 4 glasses. Adjust vodka quantities to your liking or leave it out altogether.

Hand-Tied Flies A Gift

Tying flies for fly-fishing is a pastime of many friends who are guides or avid anglers. I think the making of flies is a meditative activity. I was fortunate to pick up a few from a friend as gifts for this picnic.

Dinner on the Bridge

In the springtime, it is nice to hear water running. In celebration of the end of winter, we hosted a small gathering for dinner on a friend's bridge. Typically, this time of year the weather is unpredictable, and this day was no exception. An unexpected rainstorm caused us to hunker down at the barn and wait for the storm to pass. With the expansive mountain view, the bridge is an ideal spot to watch alpenglow just as the sun is about to drop out of view.

Lighter dishes are appealing at this time of year, such as fish and salad. For this meal, I made a simple tamari-maple salmon that can be made in advance and easily transported to be served outdoors either warm or cold. Strawberry Lemonade helped to keep things light, and it added a pretty pink to the table.

Jenn's Tamari-Maple Salmon

Our dear friend first made this dish for me years ago, and it has become a staple in our house. The key is to use fatty salmon and the highest-quality maple syrup. Sprinkle microgreens over the top of the fish and serve it over a fresh salad with Maple-Balsamic Dressing.

Serves 4

4 fatty salmon fillets

2 tablespoons olive oil

1 tablespoon tamari sauce

1 tablespoon pure maple syrup

Pinch of pepper

Pinch of chili flakes, optional

Microgreens

Preheat the oven to 425 degrees F. Line a baking sheet or tray with aluminum foil.

Pat dry the salmon pieces with a paper towel. Drizzle salmon with the olive oil. Drizzle with tamari and syrup. Bake for about 8 to 10 minutes. Sprinkle with pepper and chili flakes, if using. Serve over a simple salad with Maple-Balsamic Dressing and top with microgreens.

Maple-Balsamic Dressing

This dressing pairs beautifully with the flavors in the salmon.

Yields 1 1/2 cups

1/2 cup high-quality, thick balsamic vinegar

1/4 cup pure maple syrup

2 teaspoons Dijon mustard

Salt and pepper, to taste

1 cup extra virgin olive oil

Spring mix lettuce, for serving

Place vinegar, syrup, mustard, salt, and pepper in a blender. Turn on the blender and pour in the olive oil in a slow, steady stream. Blend until dressing is emulsified and smooth, about 10 to 15 seconds. Drizzle over a bed of lettuce and sprinkle with microgreens.

Strawberry Lemonade

This beverage a refreshing riff on classic lemonade. The strawberries make the drink a beautiful pink color, and floating edible pansies in the glass makes it even more special.

Serves 12

1 pound fresh strawberries, stems removed

2 cups sugar

6 cups water, divided

2 cups fresh lemon juice

Ice

Edible flowers, optional

Put the strawberries and lemon juice in a blender and purée.

In a small saucepan over medium-high heat, combine the sugar and 2 cups water, stirring often until dissolved; then remove from heat.

In a pitcher, add the strawberry mixture, syrup, and remaining water. Chill in the fridge until cool; then serve over ice. Float an edible flower in each glass, if desired.

Edible Flower Starts A Gift

Edible flower starts are a lovely favor for guests. Nasturtiums remind me of my grandmother's garden, so I planted some ahead of time to share with my friends. A perfect edible flower, nasturtiums have a slightly spicy note. You can use them on a salad or a dessert or in a drink.

You could pick up already started plants at your local nursery or buy a pack of seeds and plant them yourself, as I did here. Any edible flower start makes for a special gift, such as pansies, chives, or chamomile.

River Lunch

Before the National Park Service releases water from the dam for farmers downstream, you can safely ford the Snake River to an island where a group of local teens built a log teepee out of driftwood found on the island shore. There is an element of surprise when people are walking their dogs on the levee or floating the river, as there isn't a straight path to this teepee. This rustic shelter is an unexpected place for people to connect with nature and each other. On any given day, you may find a mother and her children, lovers, and friends; but one thing is constant, this natural art piece draws people in.

Early in the spring, I packed a picnic of simple radish sandwiches and sweets. You can easily round out this picnic with pickled vegetables from your local market. Because the island is sandy, I threw in a few blankets to have a nice place to sit. The teepee frame provided a place for us to enjoy time together and some spring sunshine on our faces.

Radish and Butter Crostini

This colorful appetizer is a staple snack in France and one of my favorite spring treats. The flavors are magic together.

Makes 10

1 French baguette

1 bunch of red radishes

Quality salted butter, such as Kerrygold

Maldon sea salt flakes

Preheat the oven to 350 degrees F.

Slice the baguette on the diagonal, place slices on a baking sheet, and bake for about 5 minutes, or until golden brown. Remove and let cool.

Meanwhile, slice the radishes thinly using a sharp knife or mandoline. Once the bread has cooled, slather with salted butter, arrange with radishes, and sprinkle with a generous amount of flaky salt.

Mini Citrus Bundt Cakes

These little treats are great on a picnic or as an afternoon treat.

Makes 12

1 cup unsalted butter, room temperature

1 1/2 cups sugar

1/4 teaspoon kosher salt

3 large eggs, room temperature

2 cups all-purpose flour, divided

1/3 cup buttermilk, divided

1 1/2 teaspoons vanilla extract

1/2 teaspoon almond extract

Zest of 1 orange

Preheat the oven to 350 degrees F. Spray the mini Bundt pans with nonstick baking spray.

In the bowl of an electric mixer fitted with a paddle attachment, beat the butter on medium-high until creamy. Add the sugar and salt, and then beat on medium-high until light and fluffy. With the mixer running, add the eggs one at a time, beating until well combined. Add 1 cup of the flour and beat on low until just combined. Add half of the buttermilk and beat until combined. Repeat with the remaining flour and buttermilk. Stir in the vanilla and almond extracts and the zest.

Divide the batter evenly among the pans; then gently tap each pan on the counter to level the batter. Bake until the cakes are golden brown and a toothpick inserted in the center comes out clean, about 25 to 30 minutes. Let the cakes cool in the pan for 5 minutes. Lastly, place the pans on a wire rack to cool completely.

Summer Season of Casual

Jackson Hole old-timers say,

"If summer falls on a weekend, let's have a picnic!" In many mountain towns, July 4th kicks off summer with a bang, and a freak snowstorm can end the season in August.

I plan for summer all year, scheduling hikes, booking pack trips, and laying out the garden. My summer celebration planning starts as early as January. When the summer months begin, I want to maximize my time outdoors with plenty of room for spontaneous adventures like a polar plunge in an alpine lake or river with water temperatures so chilly it takes my breath away, leaving me feeling invigorated.

Vibrant yellow arrowleaf balsamroot on the hillsides announces the season has arrived. Other favorite wildflowers include sticky geranium, Indian paintbrush, wild yarrow, pentstemon, columbine, and phlox. I return to the trails weekly in search of new blossoms. Inspired by mountain color combinations, I pair blue delphiniums with orange poppies and pink roses with sagebrush in bouquets for my tablescapes or as gifts for friends.

On summer evenings, I unwind by tending to the garden. I water the peas and lettuce, kale, herbs, and carrots. Hours spent in the garden weeding and harvesting makes my hands grubby, but serving food dug out of the soil is a satisfying gift on our dinner table. With bedtime disregarded, the kids enjoy grooming the ponies, and we all watch the sky turn pink. After full days of adventure, we are exhausted and ready to crumble into the sheets.

Summer Rituals

Pitch a tent in the backyard

Press flowers

Visit a flower farm

Go canoeing

Pick up driftwood on the riverbank

Tube down a creek

Pick berries for jam and pancakes

Build a fairy house and enter it into the fair

Hike to a high mountain lake

Go on a road trip

Visit a National Park

Watch fireworks

Collect rocks for painting

Ride a horse

Shop at the farmers market

Check out the county fair

Make a wildflower bouquet

Ride bikes until dark

Swim in the river

Build a campfire

Sleep under the stars

Catch a fish

Herb Garden

When the temperatures are high enough in June to plant outside, the first thing I like to do is plant an herb garden to cook out of for the entire summer. I either start seeds inside or hit up the nursery to pick up some of my favorite herbs starts. I select the vessel before I begin. I have used vintage wash bins, wheelbarrows, favorite pottery, and a cluster of smaller terra-cotta pots. After years of creating herb gardens, I know now to stick with herbs I regularly use in the kitchen. While I have been drawn to more unusual herbs such as tarragon or fennel, thyme, cilantro, parsley, basil, and dill are a must. Mint is often used in our household, but due to its spreading nature, it lives in its own pot. I place my herb garden close to the kitchen so it is easily accessible for daily cooking.

Summer Gatherings

Summer is a season of magic with little formality; it's not a time to be fussy. Spending time in the warm sun with family and friends is what summer is about. A summer table is about flexibility. I rarely use tablecloths in other seasons, but a casual linen cloth or a vintage find adds enough to elevate any outdoor experience. Al fresco dining by water, in an aspen grove, around a campfire, or in the backyard will create memories and traditions. I do not drag my finest china to an outdoor picnic but instead seek out unique enamelware and bamboo plates that can be gussied up to reflect the event; I pour ice-cold drinks into chic metal cups. Even tossing a blanket on the ground with a picnic can be a treasured time.

I lean to nature for table enhancements like collected river rocks, wildflowers, and found feathers.

Bugs are always a nuisance during this season, so I pack outdoor incense or a citronella and lavender candle to help ward them off.

The sun stays out late, so we can have lingering dinners under the stars and conversation can continue well past bedtime.

Pasture Fiesta

One of things I love about our property is having my horses in the backyard, something I dreamt about as a young cowgirl and now a lucky experience that my daughter gets to enjoy. Being able to hear Press and Darby whinny for breakfast and watching them eat hay while sipping my cup of coffee starts the day off perfectly.

Most evenings, we end up out with the horses, whether we are grooming them, leading them around the field in a halter, or taking a small ride around the neighborhood. I love to be surrounded by the smells of grass and the sounds of the ponies. This is a special place to eat a meal. The kids have the freedom to run around, and there is always an insane alpenglow sunset out there.

I took a small table out to the middle of the pasture, which is surrounded by 360-degree mountain views, with my favorite being Munger Mountain. Since my family loves Mexican food, likely due to spending many spring breaks south of the border, I made shrimp tacos and grilled corn in the husk for this picnic. After laughter and stories, and with full bellies, we reflected on our time together as the sun set and turned the sky pink.

Honey Panko Shrimp

These honey panko shrimp are a crowd pleaser and taste delicious in a taco with a simple aioli and jalapeño slices, or whatever toppings you love.

Serves 4–6

1/2 cup honey

1/4 cup sugar

Juice of 1 lemon plus 1 teaspoon zest

3 cups all-purpose flour, divided

1 1/2 teaspoons salt

2 eggs, beaten

1 cup water

2 teaspoons baking powder

2 cups panko breadcrumbs

2 cups shredded coconut

1 pound peeled and deveined raw medium shrimp

Vegetable oil, for deep-frying

8 corn tortillas

Garnishes (optional): avocado, sliced radishes, cilantro, fresh jalapeños

Mango-Habanero Aioli (optional, see page 119)

Line a baking sheet with parchment paper.

In a medium saucepan, combine honey, sugar, lemon juice and zest. Bring to a simmer stirring constantly, and simmer for 2 minutes, until the sugar dissolves. Remove from the heat and set aside.

In a small bowl, combine 2 cups flour and the salt.

In a second bowl, whisk together the eggs, water, remaining flour, and baking powder.

In a third bowl, combine the panko and coconut.

Make an assembly line with the three bowls. Dredge the shrimp through the flour mixture, then the egg mixture, and finally the panko mixture. Place the finished shrimp on a parchment-lined baking sheet and freeze for 30 minutes.

In a large cast-iron skillet, add 3 inches of oil. Heat the oil to 350 degrees F, then fry the shrimp until golden brown, about 3 minutes per side. Transfer to a paper towel–lined plate.

Drizzle shrimp with the honey sauce, and assemble tacos on grilled tortillas with your desired toppings.

Serve with optional Mango-Habanero Aioli.

Mango–Habanero Aioli

Makes 2 cups

1 cup frozen mango chunks

2 tablespoons fresh lime juice

1 teaspoon sugar

1 teaspoon smoked paprika

1 teaspoon curry powder

1 teaspoon smoked salt

1/2 teaspoon cayenne pepper

1/2 teaspoon black pepper

1 small habanero chili, seeded and chopped

1 cup mayonnaise

Place the frozen mango chunks, lime juice, sugar, paprika, curry powder, salt, cayenne pepper, black pepper, and habanero in a food processor and process until smooth, about 1 minute. Stir together the mango mixture and mayonnaise in a medium bowl. Cover and refrigerate until ready to use.

Grilled Corn in the Husk

Serves 6–8

6–8 ears of fresh sweet corn

Butter

Salt

Preheat grill to 375 to 450 degrees F.

Peel the husks back and remove all the silks. Replace the husks on the ears of corn and soak in water for 20 minutes. Cook the corn on the grill for about 22 minutes, rotating it to get nice grill marks. Remove from grill and slather in butter; sprinkle with salt.

Ranch Water

This is a drink I had years ago in Marfa, Texas. It is simple, light, and delicious. You're welcome.

Fresh lime juice, plus slices for garnish

Finishing salt

Ice

Casamigos Blanco Tequila

Topo Chico

Using slices of fresh lime, coat the rim of each glass with juice. Place the rim of the glass in the finishing salt. Fill the glass with ice, fresh lime juice, tequila, and Topo Chico to your liking.

Finishing Salt A Gift

You can rim a glass with this salt mixture or add it to chicken or fish.

Makes 2 cups

2 cups of flaky sea salt (I prefer Maldon)

Zest of 2 oranges

Zest of two limes

2 tablespoons smoked chili powder

Preheat oven to 225 degrees F. Line a pan with parchment paper.

Combine all the ingredients in a large bowl and whisk to mix; make sure there are no clumps. Spread the mixture evenly over the parchment. Bake for 60 minutes, or until the salt feels dry. Allow salt to dry completely and then pour into a glass container with a lid. Will store for one month.

Argentine Supper

A few years ago, some girlfriends and I learned to play polo. There is a polo club just up the street from my house, and for a few months each summer the field fills with families, pros, and grooms from all over the world. As Paul Von Gontard, founder of the club, always says, "They come for the polo and stay for the party."

Asados, which are traditional Argentine meals of beef cooked over a fire that feed a crowd, are regular occurrences at the club. My friends Poncho and Marcos are always at the fire cooking the meat, chatting with pals, and passing steak bites from a giant fork for people to sample before the meal is served.

The Villanuevas have become dear friends, and we eat meals with them regularly. At one barn party, they made a pollo disco. This is a delicious tomato stew with chicken and vegetables that is cooked in a metal disc over an open fire. While the meal is cooking, the kids practice with foot mallets on the polo field and often come to dredge a piece of bread through the bubbling sauce as an appetizer. The adults sit around the old picnic table sipping Fernet (an herbal and bitter digestif) and Coke—Marcos's favorite drink—and catch up on the latest polo gossip. As the sun sets and our meal winds down, the karaoke machine emerges for a round of 1990s country classics while we stay warm around the fire.

Pollo Disco

A *pollo disco* (chicken and vegetable stew) became a monthly tradition during the summer when the Villanuevas return. It is a simple dish cooked over an open fire and serves a crowd. There is no real recipe for this dish. You can be flexible with the vegetables and quantities. Any metal disc or oversized wok will work. Dredge some fresh bread through the sauce while it is bubbling, and you will understand why it is so delicious.

Serves 10–12

Carrots, roughly chopped

Sweet potatoes, roughly chopped

Yellow onion, roughly chopped

Mushrooms

Peas

Corn on the cob, cut in half

Chicken pieces, skin on

Tomato sauce

2 cans light beer

Oregano

Paprika

Salt and pepper

Crusty bread, for serving

Build a charcoal and wood fire in a safe place. Let the wood and coals get hot.

Place a large disc or wok over the flames. Add all the ingredients. Cover with tomato sauce and beer. Cook for two hours over the open fire, stirring occasionally and stoking the fire. To serve, ladle heaps of vegetables and chicken onto each plate and serve with crusty bread.

Simple Green Salad

While a salad is not necessary, I like to serve a very simple one with a lemon–olive oil dressing.

Serves 10

2 pounds of spring greens

Zest and juice of 2 lemons

2 tablespoons olive oil

Salt

Toss the greens in a bowl.

Make a dressing of lemon zest and freshly squeezed juice, olive oil, and salt to taste. Mix in a jar and drizzle over the greens.

Chimichurri A Gift

This classic Argentine sauce comes together easily and is a flavorful hostess gift. I drizzle it on meat, bread, and vegetables.

Makes 2 cups

1 shallot, diced

1 Fresno chili, finely chopped

3–4 garlic cloves, finely chopped

1/2 cup red wine vinegar

1 teaspoon salt

1 cup finely chopped cilantro

1/4 cup finely chopped flat-leaf parsley

2 tablespoons finely chopped fresh oregano

3/4 cup olive oil

Combine shallot, chili, garlic, vinegar, and salt in a medium bowl. Let sit for 10 minutes. Stir in cilantro, parsley, and oregano. Using a fork, whisk in oil. Transfer 1/2 cup of chimichurri to a glass jar with a lid. Adorn the jar with ribbon or a leather string.

Campout

The first time I slept in a wall tent was for two months during a summer in my twenties, at a ranch. I had no running water or toilet, so I had to tromp over to the main house to use their amenities. This semi-permanent canvas tent with a pole structure is often used by outfitters at hunting camps. My experience in this dwelling was both romantic and rustic—imagine listening to the rain on the canvas ceiling and feeling the wind through the walls. I covered myself in layers of down and wool to stay warm while wearing fleece base layers to endure the cold summer nights with no wood stove or heat. My headlamp along with candlelight on my bedside table made it possible to read when the sun went down. I often fell fast asleep, exhausted from youthful days, comforted by the noise of the wind.

Since then, I have set up a wall tent in the early summer that remains through Labor Day. The primitive dwelling is used as guest quarters, for children's campouts, and, in this case, a getaway for Mac and me. While we are close to home, the tent feels far enough away for a quiet retreat, so we take advantage as often as possible.

By dragging out furniture and plush bedding, this camping experience is elevated to glamping. A desk, side chair, and trunk make it feel more like a styled room than a simple canvas tent. Natural décor foraged from the nearby woods adds to the romance of the temporary dwelling. By a small fire burning outside, we sip coffee and enjoy some homemade granola before heading home to tend to the daily chores.

Nut and Seed Granola

This recipe is a favorite in our family. Because the granola is packed with protein, it can double as an energy-boosting trail snack when you are on the go.

Makes 6 cups

2 cups halved raw pecans

2 cups sliced almonds

1 cup raw cashews

1 cup raw pepitas

1/2 cup hemp seeds

1/2 cup flax seeds

1 cup unsweetened coconut flakes

1 tablespoon ground cinnamon

2 pinches of salt

1/3 cup high-quality maple syrup

2/3 cup coconut oil

Preheat the oven to 300 degrees F. Line a baking sheet with parchment paper.

In a large bowl, combine pecans, almonds, cashews, pepitas, hemp seeds, flax seeds, and coconut flakes. Sprinkle with cinnamon and salt. Combine all the ingredients well and set aside.

In a small saucepan over low heat, combine the maple syrup and coconut oil, stirring often. Once melted, pour over the dry ingredients, and mix well until everything is completely coated. Spread the granola onto the lined baking sheet in an even layer and press down using the back of a wooden spoon. Bake for 35 to 40 minutes, or until golden brown.

Allow the granola to cool on the baking sheet for 10 to 15 minutes, then break it apart and transfer to large Mason jars. Granola will store for up to ten days.

Pressed Flowers A Gift

Collecting wildflowers when they are at their peak is a treasure hunt. I like to inspect each bloom to ensure I harvest the flowers with the most petals, unique leaves, and an overall beautiful shape. This old-time ritual is something my grandmother taught me as a child, and it's fun to do with children. The blooms last for a very long time and can be used in décor, craft projects, or just left in a book to stumble upon later.

Supplies

Flowers

Snips

Parchment paper

Heavy book

Select your flowers from the wild, your own yard, or a local florist.

Cut the flower stems to your desired length. Fold a piece of parchment paper in half so it will cover the flowers. Place the blooms between two pieces of parchment paper. Slip the parchment-covered flowers between pages of the heavy book and leave for several days to dry and cure.

Once the flowers are dried, you could arrange them in a glass frame, laminate them to make a bookmark, or just slip them inside a favorite book.

Peony Picking

Small flower farms are popping up all over the West. A friend, Kathy Bressler, owns a peony farm down a quiet street, where my family goes to harvest every summer. Peonies are particularly hardy for our climate and grow beautifully as cut flowers because their foliage remains lovely even after the blooms are cut. You can grab a pre-picked bundle from the front porch or wander the rows yourself in search of the perfect combination. My favorite varieties are 'Sarah Berhardt', with its light pink blooms, and 'Bowl of Cream', which is a gorgeous white.

I loaded up the kids on a sunny summer afternoon for a picnic among the peonies. We snacked on homemade blackberry hand pies and a fresh ginger soda, which are both easily transported in a picnic basket. We brought our favorite clippers and a bucket for our arrangement. Unlike most flower arranging, where you mix a variety of blooms, I prefer to keep peonies simpler, with fewer colors. A bouquet in related shades is striking whether in full bloom, wilting, or past its prime.

Blackberry Hand Pies

Hand pies are an easy and quick alternative to a fruit crisp or berry pie, made even easier by using puff pastry. This recipe uses fresh blackberries, but you can use any fresh or frozen berry you prefer. This dessert is easily packed in a picnic and can be enjoyed warm or cooled.

Makes 8 pies

2 cups blackberries

2/3 cup granulated sugar

Zest and juice of 2 lemons

1 tablespoon cornstarch

Puff pastry, thawed

1 egg, lightly beaten

1/4 cup turbinado sugar

Preheat oven to 400 degrees F. Line a sheet pan with parchment paper.

In a large bowl, combine the berries, sugar, zest, and lemon juice. Once combined, sprinkle the berries with cornstarch. On a floured surface, roll out the puff pastry and cut it evenly into 8 squares. Place the fruit mixture in the middle of each square.

Fold each pastry over the fruit and crimp the pie edges together using the back of a fork. Brush the lightly beaten egg on top of the pies. Place pies on the paper-lined baking sheet. Bake for 15 minutes. Cool and enjoy.

Ginger Shrub with Lemon

This tangy vinegar syrup is wonderful with any bubbly water. Serve with fresh lemon slices.

Makes 1 bottle

4 inches unpeeled fresh gingerroot

1 cup sugar

2 lemons, more for serving

1 cup apple cider vinegar

Bubbly water, for serving

Cut up the unpeeled gingerroot and add it to a mixing bowl. Cover with the sugar.

Wash and peel the lemons, adding rinds to the bowl. Juice the lemons into the bowl. Mix ingredients, cover with plastic wrap, and let sit at room temperature for 48 hours.

Remove plastic wrap and stir the ingredients. Add the apple cider vinegar and combine until the sugar is dissolved. Discard the ginger and lemon pieces. Strain into your glass bottle. Serve over ice with bubbly water and a lemon slice. Will last in the fridge for up to two months.

Peony Arrangement A Gift

Peonies in season are my favorite flowers to work with. To make your arrangement interesting, try including a few stems of leaves and unopened buds along with different shades of flowers.

Supplies

Flowers

Snips

Vessel with cool water

Because the blooms are so large, I like to pack them tightly in the vessel, removing any greenery that will be in water to reduce bacteria. As a general guideline, the flowers should be one and a half times the height of your container. While flower frogs are making a comeback, I use chicken wire or floral foam to make my arrangement stay put if using a wider vessel. Changing the water daily will ensure the flowers last as long as possible—although, I keep them in the vase well past their prime and love to see them change shape.

Fall Season of Change

Fall tends to come on strong each year, like a new love, uprooting the lazy rhythm of summer. With the hopes of a long, colorful Indian summer, and the kids going back to school, we swap sandals for the comfort of boots and cutoffs for long pants and chunky wool sweaters. A more natural rhythm settles in as the season shifts; however, life in the mountains never ends up being this simple.

The morning air begins to cool, and the chores seem to pile on as winter rapidly approaches. There are trees to fell, buck, and split for firewood; garlic to dig up, dry, and replant; and gardens to cut back. The horses are taken to their milder winter pasture 90 miles northeast. At times, these rituals of the season's change can become overwhelming, especially if snow comes earlier than expected.

Counterbalancing the heavy outdoor work of this season, I relish the labors of love playing out in my kitchen, where I spend hours preserving—canning tomato sauce, crab apple butter, and pickled fresh vegetables from the garden to enjoy through the coming winter. My body begins to crave hearty soups and breads. Evening walks down the dirt road with the dogs and playing games with the family turn into quieter nights at home, and cozy nesting.

Fall Rituals

Rake the yard

Preserve tomato sauce

Preserve crab apple butter

Chop and stack firewood with the kids

Carve a pumpkin and roast the seeds

Work on a puzzle

Meditate before the sunrise

Pickle cabbage, fennel, carrots, and kohlrabi

Go on a trail ride

Light candles at dinner and breakfast

Watch the sunset by the river

Harvest onions and garlic and replant seed garlic

Cut back the garden and dry the flowers

Slow down

Drink warm apple cider from a thermos

Make spiritual kindling and write a message of gratitude

Go to bed early

Walk after supper

Fire Cider Tonic

Every fall when the kids go back to school, I make a batch of fire cider, an herbal elixir similar to a wellness shot commonly found at juiceries around the country. I harvest parsley, rosemary, garlic, and onion from my garden before the frost. I add other vegetables from the farmers market along with local honey. The vinegar adds a probiotic punch. My family takes a shot of this healthy tonic each morning. While the recipe can be modified to your liking, below is my go to.

1/2 cup thinly sliced fresh ginger

1/2 cup peeled, diced fresh horseradish

1 head garlic, cloves smashed and peeled

3 sprigs of rosemary

Handful of parsley

Habanero peppers cut lengthwise

1 teaspoon whole black peppercorns

1/2 small onion, cut into pieces

1 lemon, cut into pieces

1/2 orange, cut into pieces

3 tablespoons turmeric

1/3 cup honey, local if possible

4 cups raw, unfiltered apple-cider vinegar, plus more as needed

In a 1 quart vessel with a sealable, airtight lid, place all of the ingredients. After pressing everything down, submerge with vinegar, leaving a 1/2 inch at the top. Seal the jar and store in a cool, dark place, agitating every day or two. After 3 weeks, s train through a cheesecloth or a fine-mesh sieve and discard the solids. Store the tonic in a sealed container in the refrigerator up to 1 month.

Fall Gatherings

Autumn is my favorite season to entertain outdoors. I wander the trails in search of dried plants and interesting branches to incorporate into tablescapes and home décor. Hops foraged from a ranch fence will be hung on chandeliers to bring nature inside. When the hydrangeas in my planters freeze, I'll cut them at the base and place the faded blooms in an oversized container for a stunning centerpiece.

Intimate dinner parties with thoughtful menus are a welcome change after the larger barbecue gatherings of summer. Textures of wool and wood reflect the rustic simplicity of this season of abundance. I base my color choices on the changing landscape to include brown and green tones. Tossing an unexpected textile such as a Pendleton blanket or vintage Navajo rug on the table in place of a traditional tablecloth sets the tone for a casual, no-fuss gathering. Flickering candlelight creates a romantic atmosphere.

Common fall gifts for my guests include crab apple butter, spiritual kindling, and a handmade candle. Some call these homemade accents parting gifts, but because we live at 6,000 plus feet above sea level, I call them elevated gifts.

Wood Gathering Supper

Chop wood and it will warm you twice, the saying goes.

When crimson and burnt sienna leaves litter the roads, I start thinking about gathering wood to heat our home for the long Wyoming winter. We pull on Carhartt overalls, I fill thermoses with steaming hot cider, and our family piles into the ranch truck and heads to the forest. The chainsaw squeaks and the smell of gas tickles the back of my throat as my husband, Mac, fires her up after a year's rest. After we fill the bed of the pickup with the cut and split rounds, we admire our hard work, enjoy our refreshments, and head home to stack the wood in our backyard. This is a day when we all work up an appetite and need a quick, satisfying meal to fill our hungry bellies.

In the fall, my family requests pasta often—specifically, pasta puttanesca. This recipe of simple, garlicky tomato sauce gains an elevated complexity with ingredients found in the pantry— capers, anchovies, and olives. I always add heaps of fresh flat-leaf parsley and a few dashes of red pepper flakes for some heat. This fragrant pasta was said to be made first by the "ladies of the night" to attract customers; but present day, my family comes running every time I serve it.

Pasta Puttanesca

This simple and delicious pasta is perfect for the change of season when your body begins to crave heartier meals. While any pasta will do, I prefer thick spaghetti or linguine. This recipe is ridiculously easy and will serve a crowd.

Serves 6

3 tablespoons olive oil, divided

5 cloves garlic, lightly smashed and peeled

3 anchovy fillets

1 28-ounce can whole plum tomatoes

1/2 cup pitted black olives

2 tablespoons capers (more for serving)

Crushed red pepper flakes to taste

1 pound linguine or thick spaghetti

Salt and freshly ground pepper to taste

Freshly chopped parsley, oregano, and basil for garnish

Pecorino cheese for garnish

In a heavy skillet, add 2 tablespoons olive oil, garlic, and anchovies; cook over medium-to-low heat until the garlic is lightly golden, stirring occasionally.

Add the tomatoes and crush them with the back of a wooden spoon. Raise the heat to medium, stirring occasionally until the tomatoes break down and becomes saucy, about 10 minutes. Stir in olives, capers, and red pepper flakes. Let simmer until the pasta is ready.

Cook pasta in boiling salty water, stirring occasionally, until it is tender. Drain pasta and serve with sauce and remaining 1 tablespoon oil. Taste and adjust seasonings as desired. Garnish with fresh herbs and pecorino cheese.

Pear and Bourbon Skillet Cake

This old-fashioned way of cooking in iron is versatile for all kinds of gatherings. The skillet also makes a beautiful serving piece.

Serves 8 to 10

1 cup all-purpose flour

3/4 teaspoon cardamom

3/4 teaspoon baking powder

1/4 teaspoon kosher salt

2 large eggs, room temperature

3/4 cup granulated sugar

3 tablespoons bourbon

1/2 teaspoon vanilla extract

1/3 cup well-shaken buttermilk, at room temperature

3 medium pears

1 stick unsalted butter, melted and cooled, plus more for greasing the pan

1 tablespoon turbinado sugar

Confectioners' sugar for dusting

Preheat the oven to 350 degrees F. Fit a 9-inch cast-iron skillet snuggly with a piece of parchment paper or grease it with butter.

In a bowl, whisk together the flour, cardamom, baking powder, and salt. In a separate large bowl, beat the eggs until foamy. Whisk in the granulated sugar, bourbon, and vanilla extract. Pour in the buttermilk and then combine.

Peel, core, and halve 2 1/2 of the pears and cut them into cubes. Reserve the remaining half pear, unpeeled, and cut it into 1/4-inch slices to decorate the top.

Add half the flour mixture to the wet ingredients, stirring just until combined; then gently fold in half the melted butter. Repeat with remaining flour mixture and melted butter. Lastly, fold in the cubed pear.

Transfer batter to the skillet and arrange the pear slices in a circular pattern on top of the batter. Sprinkle with the turbinado sugar. Bake until the cake turns a deep golden brown and a knife inserted in the center comes out clean, 55 to 65 minutes. Transfer skillet to a cooling rack and let sit for 5 minutes.

The cake can be served warm or at room temperature directly from the skillet; whichever you choose, make sure to dust it with confectioners' sugar before serving.

Trail Ride Repast

Twice a week, a rotating group of friends meet at various trailheads to spend a day in the mountains on horseback. On the last ride of the season, the rattle of my 1990s hand-me-down trailer, loaded with my two whinnying palominos, announces my arrival. A gourmet picnic balances on the back seat between my mom's old western saddle and buckets of grain.

I grab my picnic supplies from the back of the truck and get to work setting up the table before the girls arrive. The colors of alpenglow and my favorite vintage Navajo blankets inspire the tablescape. I fill a 1940s family trophy pitcher with a loose bouquet of garden flowers, a humble mix of echinacea, Astrantia, dead hops, and serviceberries. I made crab apple butter as a gift, which is our high-altitude fruit option.

After tacking the horses, we ride through a grassy sage meadow that was left to grow tall during the hot summer months and head towards the mountains. In an aspen grove, leaves every shade of yellow and green have blanketed the trail. Sleeping Indian, Jackson Peak, and the valley below all come into view. We ride for a couple of hours then return to our trailers to celebrate the end of the season.

While the girls untack horses, I pull out our picnic. I have prepared delicata squash, simple charcuterie, chai-spiced apple galette, and a basic cocktail of sage simple syrup and Wyoming whiskey. As the horses graze around us, we gather around the table, toast these fleeting autumn evenings, and gobble up supper while continuing conversations of the day.

The full moon rises, and the Sleeping Indian begins to glow pink; we cozy up in Navajo blankets, not wanting the evening to end. But alas, the ponies need to get home.

Roasted Delicata Squash with Almonds and Olives

Nothing beats this sweet squash in the fall. I cut the squash into circles before cooking, which makes for a beautiful shape. You can grill the squash over an open fire or sauté, but here I roast them to get the nice brown color on the circles.

Serves 6

2 delicata squash, seeds removed and cut into ½-inch slices

3 tablespoons extra virgin olive oil

1/2 teaspoon minced red habanero chili

1/4 cup golden raisins

1/3 cup apple cider vinegar

1 large lime, juiced

4 tablespoons honey

Salt and pepper to taste

5 or 6 fresh sage leaves, very thinly sliced

2 tablespoons Marcona almonds, toasted

1/2 cup Castelvetrano olives, cut in half

Preheat the oven to 375 degrees F. Line a baking sheet with parchment paper.

Place the prepared squash in a large bowl and coat with the oil. Season with salt and pepper and toss. Transfer the squash to the prepared baking sheet and arrange in a single layer. Roast until golden brown, 15 minutes per side.

In a small saucepan, add the habanero, golden raisins, vinegar, lime juice, and honey and bring to a boil. Add a pinch of salt and pepper. Reduce heat to low and simmer until the mixture is syrupy, 10 minutes. Just before serving, spoon the sauce over the squash. Toss with the sage, almonds, and olives.

Grazing Board

When hosting guests, there is no easier way to display your favorite snacks then on a grazing board. To make your board stunning, pick a color palette. For fall, a mix of warm tones, deep reds, and faded greens is lovely. Start with the bigger items like the cheese, crackers, and meats; then fill in with the more delicate items like pears, apples, nuts, and jam.

Cheeses

Aged cheddar cheese

Wedge of blue cheese

Merlot BellaVitano cheese

Brie or goat cheese

Fresh Fall Flavors

Figs

Apples

Pears

Black grapes

Rosemary to separate items

Meats

Prosciutto

Salami

Local game sausage

Round It Out

Crackers of various sizes and colors

Fig jam

Candied nuts

Green olives

Apple Galette

A simple fruit dessert is what I gravitate to most seasons. Just mix up the star ingredient based on what is in season.

Serves 8 to 10

1/2 cup maple syrup

3 tablespoons salted butter

1 teaspoon ground cinnamon

1/2 teaspoon ground ginger

1/4 teaspoon ground cardamom

1/4 teaspoon allspice

1/4 teaspoon freshly grated nutmeg

1/8 teaspoon ground black pepper

1 teaspoon vanilla extract

1 pinch flaky sea salt

1 sheet frozen puff pastry, thawed

1/2 cup whole milk ricotta cheese

4–5 Honeycrisp apples, halved, cored, and thinly sliced

Turbinado sugar, for sprinkling

Ice cream or whipped cream, for serving

Preheat the oven to 400 degrees F. Line a baking sheet with parchment paper.

Bring the maple syrup, butter, cinnamon, ginger, cardamom, allspice, nutmeg, and pepper to a boil in a small saucepan over high heat; then lower heat and simmer 2 minutes. Remove from heat. Stir in vanilla extract and a pinch of salt.

On a lightly floured surface, roll out the puff pastry into a rectangle about 1/4 inch thick. Place the pastry on the parchment-lined baking sheet and spread the ricotta evenly over the pastry, leaving a 1-inch border.

Drizzle the ricotta with 2 tablespoons of the spiced maple sauce. Arrange the apples, skin-side up, over the ricotta. Drizzle the apples with 2 to 3 tablespoons of the maple sauce. Fold the edges of the pastry up and over the apples. Brush the edges of the pastry with the remaining maple sauce and sprinkle with sugar.

Transfer to the oven and bake for 25 to 35 minutes, or until golden brown. It is okay if the edges get dark. Let cool slightly then serve plain or with ice cream or whipped cream.

Spiced Crab Apple Butter A Gift

Wyoming's climate is a bit too harsh for most fruit trees to thrive, so crab apple trees are my favorite fruiting option. It is a family affair to pick the tiny sour apples off the branches to preserve, eating a few along the way. Select crab apples that are fresh, ripe, firm, and blemish free. The beautiful red color makes crab apple butter a showstopper as a gift. Preserving it in wide-mouth jars makes it ea easy to scoop out. For the presentation, I cover the top of the lid with a piece of colorful fabric, leather, or muslin and tie it with a piece of ribbon, twine, or leather lacing.

Serves 6 to 8

4–6 pounds of crab apples, washed and quartered, with seeds

1 cup water

4 cups pure cane sugar

2 teaspoons cinnamon

1/2 teaspoon cloves

Place the crab apples in a large saucepan, add 1 cup of water, and heat until simmering. Cook until apples are softened, stirring often to prevent them from sticking to the pan. Run apples through a food mill and return to the saucepan; add the sugar and spices, adjusting to taste.

Slowly simmer the crab apple butter until it reaches your desired thickness (fruit butters usually have a thick, creamy, spreadable consistency). Stir occasionally to prevent scorching. Once the butter has cooled, ladle into jars and seal. If you are quick canning, it will last in your fridge for up to two weeks. If you are water bath canning to add to your pantry, follow along on page 179.

Water Bath Canning for Preservation

Once your water is boiling, cure your jars in the boiling water for ten minutes. Remove and strain water. Ladle crab apple butter into clean, warm, prepared jars, leaving 1/2 inch head space from the top of the jar. Wipe the rim of the jar with a clean cloth. Follow manufacturer's instructions for preparing lids; then place lids onto the jars, making sure the seal meets the rim. Screw on the metal rings. Place your jars into the pot of boiling water, submerging fully. Process your crab apple butter for 20 minutes.

Remove the jars, place them on a cooling rack or dry kitchen towel two inches apart. Leave for 2 to 3 hours to cool completely, then tighten the bands. Wash the film off the outside of the jars and store in a cool place until use.

The Ritual of the Rut

Before moving to Wyoming, I knew very little about wildlife, specifically elk, bison, or moose. The first time my parents loaded the family into our 1990 Suburban with a collection of scratchy blankets, a simple picnic of soup, bread, and hot chocolate in a thermos to watch the annual elk rut, I didn't exactly understand what we were going to witness.

As the sun lowered, we drove north from our home in Teton Village along the rough and winding Moose-Wilson road towards the Death Canyon trailhead and the historic White Grass Ranch. Armed with binoculars, we were in search of the rutting elk. My mom explained that the rut happens every fall when the local elk herd descends from their high-altitude summer feed grounds and the bull elk display their dominance to "collect a harem of cow elk." The bulls bugle to make their presence known and defend their prizes—cow elk—by sparring off other bull elk. Seeing this up close was exceptional. The high-pitched bugle sent chills down my spine and the sparring seemed so rough, I was worried for the bulls' safety.

We watched this display of nature until the sky turned from pink to black and the stars were shining. Since then, I have made it a ritual to load up the ranch truck and pack a picnic, wool blankets, and binoculars and head to Grand Teton National Park in search of these bugling beauties. Their calls now signify the shift in season.

Roasted Chicken Thighs with Shallots and Grapes

I make roasted chicken thighs in various forms weekly. This healthy and quick skillet dish is sure to be added to your family's rotation. Bonus: it is easy to transport to any outdoor location.

Serves to 4 to 6

6 skin-on chicken thighs

Olive oil

2 cloves garlic, finely diced

Salt and freshly ground black pepper

2 shallots, quartered

2 cups purple and green grapes

1 tablespoon unsalted butter

Thyme sprigs plus some thyme leaves for garnish

Preheat oven to 425 degrees F.

In a large bowl, toss the chicken with 3 tablespoons olive oil and garlic. Season well with salt and pepper.

Place the shallots and grapes in a heated skillet; toss gently with 2 tablespoons olive oil and season well with salt. Rub butter under the chicken skin then nestle the chicken skin-side up in among the shallots and grapes and lay the thyme sprigs on top of the mixture. Roast for 25 to 30 minutes, until the chicken is cooked through and the shallots and grapes have begun to soften and caramelize. Turn the oven to broil. Discard the thyme sprigs and broil the chicken for 1 to 2 minutes, until the skin is crispy and golden. Remove from oven, scatter fresh thyme leaves on the top, and serve.

Fig and Burning Sage Simple Syrup

Fig and sage are a perfect pair for the change of the season. This simple syrup can elevate any beverage. Add it to iced tea, Topo Chico, or even a hot toddy.

Makes 1 *pint jar*

1 cup water

1 cup sugar

3 fresh figs, halved

8 fresh sage leaves, halved

In a medium saucepan, combine the water and sugar. Bring to a simmer over medium heat, stirring often, until sugar has dissolved. Add the halved figs and sage leaves and simmer for 1 minute. Remove from heat and allow ingredients to steep for 30 minutes to 1 hour.

Remove the figs and sage leaves and discard. Transfer the cooled syrup to a canning jar with a lid. Can be stored in the fridge for up to 3 weeks.

Roasted Hazelnut and Milk Chocolate Chip Skillet Cookie

Before moving to Wyoming, I lived in Oregon, where hazelnuts were abundant and we cooked with them often. Anytime I can incorporate them into my baking, I do. This is a delicious skillet cookie with nuts and sweetness in every bite.

Serves 4 to 6

1 cup unsalted butter

1 cup brown sugar

1/2 cup granulated sugar

2 eggs, whisked

1 teaspoon vanilla extract

2 cups plus 2 tablespoons flour

1 teaspoon baking soda

1/2 teaspoon salt

3/4 cup milk chocolate chunks

3/4 cup semi-sweet chocolate chips

1/2 cup coarsely chopped roasted hazelnuts

Fresh whipped cream or ice cream, if desired

Preheat oven to 325 degrees F.

In a 10-inch cast-iron skillet, melt butter over medium heat, stirring often, until it starts to bubble and is completely melted. Turn heat to low and add both sugars, stirring well. Continue stirring until smooth and glossy. Chill in the fridge or freezer for 10 to 15 minutes.

Retrieve skillet, add eggs and vanilla, and stir well. Stir in flour, baking soda, and salt. Be sure the dough is not warmer than room temperature before adding the chocolate; then mix in chocolate chunks and chips and stir to combine.

Bake for 25 minutes, or until the edges are light golden brown. The inside will still be slightly gooey. Cut into wedges and serve warm. Add an optional dollop of whipped cream or a scoop of ice cream.

Ceremony Candle A Gift

With grounding scents of smoke and earth, this combination of clary sage, cedarwood, and palo santo is inspired by cleansing rituals around the world. Fall is great time to set intentions for the upcoming winter, and your guests will be delighted with this ceremonial token.

Makes 6 candles

Supplies

Pre-tabbed candlewicks

6 (8-ounce) pottery or glass containers

Pencil

2 pounds organic soy wax

Candy thermometer

Essential oils of clary sage, cedar wood, palo santo

Bandana or muslin fabric

Leather lacing or ribbon

Securely attach the pre-tabbed wick to the center bottom of your container. Once the wick is secure, wrap the top of the wick around a pencil and rest the pencil across top of the container so the wick is standing upright.

Melt the wax in a double boiler and heat it to 185 degrees F. Remove from the heat and add drops of essential oils to your liking. Stir the oils for 2 full minutes (it is important to blend well). Once the wax has cooled to 140 degrees F, pour the melted wax into the containers, leaving a half inch at the top. Allow the wax to cool undisturbed overnight. The scent profile will be best if you let the candles cure for 10 days.

To package, wrap in a bandana or ripped muslin fabric and secure with a loose 4-way knot on the top. Finish the look with a hangtag or a personal message. I think packaging is as important as the gift itself, so get creative and experiment with different materials.

Handcrafted Gifts

As a young child, I spent time making things by hand with generations in my family. This tradition fueled my love to give handmade gifts at my gatherings. Now, my guests have come to look forward to some type of favor, or parting gift. Following are some of my ideas for takeaway mementos made using natural ingredients or components. They can each be adapted to your particular taste; make them your own.

Infused Oils

Infusions are a wonderful way to capture the beauty and flavor in herbs, spices, and citrus. I use a variety of ingredients to suit the season or recipient. A few of my favorite ingredients include garlic cloves, red pepper flakes, thyme, rosemary, dried chiles, and lemon peels. These oils can be used to add flavor to eggs, vegetables, or meats.

Heat olive oil to 100 degrees in a small cast iron pot. Remove from the heat and add herbs and spices. Cover and let steep for an hour. Transfer to your favorite glass bottles using a funnel. Adorn with a simple ribbon and a sprig of rosemary. Will store in the pantry for up to a month.

Bath Salts

Bath salts make for a relaxing and beautiful gift with ingredients found at the market or in your pantry. A bath is a nice ritual that most people enjoy, especially on colder days or after a long day adventuring. In a large ceramic bowl, combine 2 cups of Epsom salt and 1 cup of Himalayan sea salt for the base of the salt mixture. Add essential oils of your choosing.

I add dried flowers to my bath salts because they add to the beauty of the gift. Please note that adding the dried flowers makes for a bit of clean up in the tub, but worth it to me.

Fill any clean glass container with the salt mixture. Jars can be purchased at a craft store or collected at vintage and secondhand shops. Wrap with a beautiful ribbon, a sprig of lavender or greens, and add a handwritten note.

Floral Salt

10–15 drops of any combination lavender, bergamot, Roman chamomile, rose, ylang-ylang, grapefruit, or geranium

1/4 cup dried flowers such as rose, lavender, or calendula

Green Salt

10–15 drops of any combination rosemary, eucalyptus, juniper, cedar, sandalwood, or peppermint

1/4 cup chopped fresh rosemary

Mulling Spices

A mulling spice mixture is a perfect gift during the holidays and very easy to make with children. This spice mix can be added to apple cider, red wine, or simmering water on the stove for a seasonal scent. Unexpected spices such as cardamom pods, whole star anise, nutmeg seeds, whole cloves, and cinnamon sticks make it unique. Dried orange slices are a festive addition. I make sachets in November and keep a stash on hand for place settings or a quick hostess gift paired with a bottle of Beaujolais or a handmade mug.

In a large bowl, mix all of the smaller ingredients together. Divide the mixture into small muslin bags and then add the larger pieces. Take a decorative piece of thin string or ribbon and tie the top shut. A handwritten card such as, "Brew sachet with a bottle of red wine or apple cider. Happy Holidays," adds a personal touch.

Herb Honey

Infusing honey is easy, and while honey is a common item in the pantry, elevating it with herbs makes it special. I like to use local honey when possible. Collecting unique jars from an antique mall or craft store will add to the presentation of this gift, but make sure the top closes securely.

Clean your glass vessels. Add dried herbs such as lavender, sage, rosemary, or thyme to the bottom of the jar. Pour honey over the top of the herbs and mix well. Present the honey wrapped in a piece of fabric or tied with a ribbon. Gift with a fresh loaf of sourdough for extra credit.

Harvested Sage Bundle

I love the smell of sagebrush and try and incorporate this aromatic, easily found plant, in most things I make. While traditionally smudge sticks are made out of white sage, which grows wild in many states and mountains, it is not native to Jackson; our sagebrush is a great alternative. I use these bundles as decoration.

I bring clippers and a basket and walk out the door to collect the longest and freshest pieces of green sage I can find. I use a piece of leather or twine to tie the bundles together. Place the sage in even piles and tie tightly with twine as shrinkage will occur when the sage dries.

Floral Tea

Having tea is an easy way to elevate a quiet moment in your day. Floral teas can be made with any dried flower from your garden or purchased from a health food store. I use rose, chamomile, and lavender, but you can get creative and experiment with herbal flavors such as sage or mint.

Place the dried flowers in a small muslin bag or tea sachet. Boil water and let the bag steep in water for 3 minutes. Remove bag and stir in a dash of sugar for sweetness. Tie the bags with a piece of twine or ribbon for easy gift giving.

Spiritual Kindling

I make spiritual kindling in the fall when fire season is upon us. I reach for a basket, head to the woods, and gather a variety of plants to bundle together. A few favorite aromatic plants that I like to include are sagebrush, juniper, and pine. If you live in a more temperate climate, grab pepper berry branches or eucalyptus. I top the bundles with a small pine cone, a piece or two of dried citrus, and a stick of palo santo.

To assemble, begin by laying two to three pieces of small kindling for the base. Then layer all of the foraged greenery in a nice pattern on top of the kindling. Top with the other accoutrements and tie securely together with a piece of twine or beautiful fabric. The kindling can be used to send intentions to the universe, celebrate a special occasion, manifest dreams, or just connect with the outdoors. I believe it creates magic.

Preserved Lemons

Preserved lemons add notes of citrus and saltiness that compliment chicken, grains or salad dressing. Through the fermentation process, the rind breaks down eliminating the bitterness. This attractive edible fruit makes for a great gift.

Makes 3 (16-ounce Weck jars)

5 Meyer lemons	Whole cloves	Salt
Black peppercorns	Cumin seeds	

Trim the tips of the lemons without exposing the flesh. Slice the lemon lengthwise into quarters without slicing through completely. Sprinkle the inside of the lemons with a generous amount of salt and pack them tightly into a glass jar. Sprinkle each lemon with additional salt and spices. Submerge the lemons in the brine and let ferment for at least a month.

For a lovely hostess gift or favor for guests, package the jars in cloth with a hangtag or note.

Natural Fire Starter

These aromatic bundles can be used as a place setting for a winter dinner party and double as a gift. I forage various greens from my yard and the forest. I embellish these fire starters with slices of dried oranges and baby pine cones. Rosemary, eucalyptus, dried flowers, and a stick of palo santo are great additions, as well.

To assemble the fire starter, arrange the materials in a nice cluster with a strong green as the base. Build upon the base by layering greens, pine cones, and dried flowers; tie the bundle together with twine. Thread the orange slice through the twine. I tell my guests to build a fire at home and add this little starter to the ritual of their fire.

Citrus Cooking Salts

These easy citrus salts are a wonderful addition to chicken or pork. They are also great sprinkled over salad and pasta. This simple, pretty, and fresh salt recipe is a great gift for foodies.

Makes 3 cups

2 cups Maldon or other flaky salt

4 tablespoons finely chopped fresh rosemary

4 tablespoon finely chopped fresh sage

4 tablespoons finely chopped fresh thyme

1 teaspoon dried lavender

Zest of 4 oranges

Preheat your oven to 225 degrees F. Spread the mixture in a thin layer on a baking sheet lined with parchment paper. Make sure to break up any clumps that may have formed. Bake for 60 minutes until the salt and herbs feel dry. They will store in an airtight vessel for up to a month.

Saddlebag Paté

A cooler of frozen chicken livers that I spotted at the farmers market inspired me to create a paté. While organ meats are not popular, the health benefits intrigued me. My saddlebag paté is rich, creamy, and inexpensive. If a farmers market is not readily available, ask at the butcher counter. My girlfriends request this treat on all our trail ride picnics.

Serves 8

8 tablespoons unsalted butter, divided

2 shallots, peeled and finely chopped

1 pound chicken livers, trimmed

2 tablespoons fresh thyme leaves

1/4 cup Madeira

5 tablespoons heavy cream

Kosher salt

In a large cast-iron skillet, melt 4 tablespoons of butter over medium heat. Add the shallots, being careful not to burn. Add the livers, thyme, and Madeira; cook on high for about 5 minutes, until the livers are lightly browned. Remove from the heat and transfer to a blender. Add the cream and the remaining 4 tablespoons of butter. Puree until smooth. Adjust seasoning according to taste. Evenly distribute the pate to small clean glass jars. Once cool, cover with lid and refrigerate until firm. Serve with crostini, onion jam, and cornichons.

Simple Bouquet

Who doesn't love to receive flowers? While flowers are a common gift, you can elevate them easily with these few tips. Grocery store flowers are a great start; add stems foraged from nature or a few special blooms from your local flower shop to add movement, height, and creativity to your arrangement. Because most people don't have extra vases lying around, a Ball jar tied with a ribbon and a handwritten note is a simple way to make a flower gift look finished. If you don't have a jar, wrap the bouquet in brown Kraft paper and tie it with leather or ribbon.

Acknowledgments

Four and a half years ago, I met with Lisa over coffee, with an idea to create an entertaining book out West. Matched by a similar enthusiasm for pretty parties, props, and our beautiful landscape, we started on an amazing creative journey. She was new to photography and I was not a writer.

Along the way, we were fortunate to have the support of many:

A big thank you to Madge Baird of Gibbs Smith publisher for saying yes to our project and for masterfully editing our book. Deepest gratitude to Leigh Reagan Smith, who taught the first writing class I took and pushed me to develop my voice. Shout out to Darla Worden, editor-in-chief of *Mountain Living*, for being a valuable cheerleader.

We were fortunate to have had renowned professional photographer Tim Clinch of Two Photographers on our team from beginning to end, processing our photos and giving endless support and wisdom from his home in Bulgaria. Thanks also to Joanna Maclennan of Two Photographers for invaluable support and friendship.

We are especially grateful to those who allowed us to shoot on their property: Astrid Flood, Kathy Bressler, Darcy Shipka, Pia Valar, the Roubins, the Linns, and Barb Trompeter.

Thank you to friends Christy Robertson, Leigh Chrisinger, Whitney Junot, the Linn family, Maeve and Macy Jane, my sister Emily, my mom Joni, the Villanueva family, Bunni Bishop, Poncho and Venecia, the creative wreath-making ladies, and the killer ice fishing crew.

We are grateful for our dog models—Shep, Scoobs, Charlie, Tato, and Maggie—and our horse models—Press, Darby, Maverick, and You Bet.

Most importantly, thanks to our families for their unwavering support of this project. Sweet Mac was the best "operations manager" and put up with shoots all over the house, shuttling kids, feeding pets, and living among piles of props and leftover food. Thomas listened to our endless phone conversations and offered great editorial advice. Our children—Izzy, Hunter (how about those fish), Sawyer, and Miller—willingly modeled and always made our shoots fun.

Thank you, Lisa, for your enthusiasm, incredible props and style, willingness to shoot anywhere, and chasing this dream with me.

Thank you, Hillary, for trusting me with your idea and inviting me into your stylish handmade world.

We had the best time creating this little gem of a book. We hope it inspires you to set a table outdoors and create a little magic.

Hillary Munro has been inspired by beautiful things her entire life. She is an entertaining and craft expert, home cook, and collector of cowboy boots. She loves to throw a great party. Her passion for the Old West and most things vintage makes her aesthetic fresh and unique. She owns a garden and home store, Graze, in Jackson, Wyoming, where she gets to use her creativity daily. She lives in Jackson with her husband, Mac, two children—Sawyer and Miller—two dogs, two horses, and a small flock of chickens. She always aims for the unexpected when entertaining and searches for beauty and magic in the everyday, while incorporating it in an approachable way. This is her first book.

Wilson, Wyoming writer and photographer Elizabeth (Lisa) Clair Flood has been telling stories out West for over twenty-five years. The author of six western design and lifestyle books, her articles have appeared in national and international publications. A San Francisco native and great-great-granddaughter of an 1849 California pioneer, Lisa is inspired by the Old West and the beauty of her current surroundings. She lives in a 1950s log cabin with her family (two dogs, a cat, two kids, and a husband) on a road she shares with mangy moose, bald eagles, people on horseback, dog walkers, and pickup trucks. Old things like rustic chairs, sweat-stained cowboy hats, and antlers clutter her place.

First Edition

28 27 26 25 24   5 4 3 2 1

Text © 2024 Hillary Munro
Photographs © 2024 Elizabeth Clair Flood
End paper illustration © 2024 Rachel Robinson

Published by
Gibbs Smith
570 N. Sportsplex Dr.
Kaysville, Utah 84037

1.800.835.4993 orders
www.gibbs-smith.com

Designed by Rita Sowins and Brynn Evans

This product is made of FSC®-certified and other controlled material.

Library of Congress Control Number: 2024930623

ISBN: 978-1-4236-6578-6